hotshots

This book belongs to
I am (Age)
People sometimes call me
(My Nickname)
I live at

For Parents

Children love things to be *happening*. Movement and noise, brightness and action generally appeal to them more than stability and silence.

The problem is that often when we try to interest children in Bible reading we don't include much *action*.

That's where this book comes in. As well as Bible text to read, it includes relevant questions, puzzles, prayers and other related things to do.

The Bible passages chosen for this Hotshots are about two periods in the history of the earth when things were really happening. The first is recorded in the book of Genesis when God's creative genius brought our world into being. It's an account to help children understand that they were deliberately created for a purpose, by a loving God. The second is in the Bible book of Acts, when people were excited by the fact that Jesus, who they thought had left them, was in fact still making things happen, by his Spirit.

This book is for children, but it's not an adult free zone. It will be hard for most children to continue to use it regularly without encouragement, so try to sit with them sometimes, or often, and read together. We hope that God becomes more real to your child through Hotshots. And wouldn't it be great if it helped the two of you to enjoy God more, together?

How would you like to meet God?

We don't mean when you die! Today!

Millions of people all over the world have a special meeting with God every day as they take time to pray and read the Bible.

God is invisible so they don't see him, but God's Spirit communicates with them.

You can read the Bible with this book in your own special meeting with God. As you read it, think about what God is telling you. God wants to communicate with you, so listen for what he is saying.

You might find it helpful to decide on a time and place where you'll do your Hotshots reading.

Write it here:

MEETING TIME:

(Colour in that time)

MEETING PLACE: hero's den

You'll need a pen or pencil and some coloured pencils. And you may want to record your own special notes on a cassette, computer or notepad to remember what God says to you.

Have fun! Just like God, the Bible is alive and active. Through meeting with God we become more alive too.

Alana

Sean

These kids made up their own club...
They call themselves...

hotshots

Meet **Kate...** their leader.

She's fun, smart, almost grown up – and just a bit whacky.

She usually looks like this...

Except when she says...

The Hotshots read the Bible...

Usually they read it in their leader's garage. That's their clubhouse.

Then the Hotshots head for the time ship parked out the back of the garage and their leader becomes...

Captain Kate

Commander of the Time-ship to Bible-land!

Would you like to join them in their adventures?

If your answer is 'YES' add your name to the Hotshots club list.

You can read the Bible with the Hotshots

This book will guide you. The parts you'll need from the Bible are printed in this book beside this sign. Sometimes you might like to ask someone to help you find them in a real Bible.

The Bible bits in this book come from different parts of the Bible, both Old and New Testaments. The very first chapter in the Old Testament tells about the time the universe exploded with energy when God made our world. The New Testament tells about the time the church 'exploded' with the energy of God.

Are you ready to hear about those exciting times?

Then let's go!

Genesis 1:1-5

The book of the Bible. You can find it in the contents.

The chapter. A big number on a Bible page.

Verses 1 to 5. The little numbers on a Bible page.

1 Things really start to move!

Have you ever wondered what things were like before God made the world?

That's where the Bible starts. The Hotshots read it with Kate.

Genesis 1:1-5

In the beginning God created the heavens and the
earth. [2] The earth was barren, with no form of life;
it was under a roaring ocean covered with darkness.
But the Spirit of God was moving over the water.
[3] God said, "I command light to shine!" And light
started shining. [4] God looked at the light and saw
that it was good. He separated
light from darkness
[5] and named the light
"Day" and the
darkness "Night".
Evening came and
then morning—that
was the first day.

Things really start to move! continued ...

After they read the Bible, the Hotshots talked about the huge difference God made. 'Isn't God awesome!' said Reuben.

'He sure is,' agreed Kate. 'Let's tell God how great we think he is. The Spirit of God who was moving in the beginning is here with us now. We can pray and God will hear us.'

Prayer Idea:
Now you've read how the world got started, why don't you tell God your thoughts about it like the Hotshots did?

2 Hey! This is good!

'Creation time!' said Kate when the Hotshots turned up at their clubhouse.

The others looked puzzled. ' God created the heavens and the earth. We can't beat that, but how about creating a mural? A creation mural!'

'Are we going to paint on the walls?' asked Mei.

''Would you like to? Dad said it's OK. He gave me this paint and some brushes.'

'Let's do it!' laughed Reuben.

'We should start with Light and Dark,' said Alana.

They painted one wall black and the one next to it white.

'Now what?' asked Sean.

They read the Bible to find out what God made next.

Genesis 1:6-10

6 God said, "I command a dome
to separate the water above it
from the water below it." 7 And
that's what happened. God made
the dome 8 and named it "Sky."
Evening came and then
morning—that was the second
day. 9 God said, "I command the
water under the sky to come
together in one place, so there
will be dry ground." And that's
what happened. 10 God named
the dry ground "Land," and he
named the water "Ocean." God
looked at what he had done and
saw that it was good.

Can you guess the three things the Hotshots painted next?

conea _ _ _ _ _

ysk _ _ _

rtahe _ _ _ _ _

Prayer:
Dear God, those things are even hard to draw. There's no way we could make them. You are amazing!

3 But wait! There's more!

'I've got some green paint,' Kate told the Hotshots. 'I think we'll be needing it today.'

Genesis 1:11-13

11 God said, "I command
the earth to produce all
kinds of plants, including fruit
trees and grain." And that's what
happened. 12 The earth produced all
kinds of vegetation. God looked at
what he had done, and it was good.
13 Evening came and then morning—
that was the third day.

Can you find ten different types of plants in this wordfind?

B	P	I	N	E	T	R	E	E
A	E	G	I	T	W	C	G	A
N	P	R	N	U	T	A	G	P
A	A	A	R	A	N	C	P	R
N	L	S	O	I	R	T	L	I
A	M	S	S	V	E	U	A	C
S	G	O	E	Y	F	S	N	O
O	D	O	T	A	M	O	T	T

They can go any way at all, even diagonally. If you want to know which words to look for there's a list on page 20.

Brainbuster Puzzle: when you have crossed off all the words, the left over letters in order tell what God thought about his creation. Write it in these boxes.

_ _   _ _ _   _ _ _ _

(The answer is on page 22)

Prayer:
Dear God, of all the plants you made I'm specially glad you made _______ and __________. Thank you.

4

It's not over yet!

The white wall of the Hotshots mural is looking interesting. What will they paint on the black wall? Read the Bible bit to find out what God made next.

Genesis 1:14-19

14 God said, "I command lights to
appear in the sky and to separate
day from night and to show the
time for seasons, special days,
and years. 15 I command them to
shine on the earth." And that's
what happened. 16 God made two
powerful lights, the brighter one
to rule the day and the other to
rule the night. He also made the
stars. 17 Then God put these lights
in the sky to shine on the earth,
18 to rule day and night, and to
separate light from darkness.
God looked at what he had done,
and it was good. 19 Evening came
and then morning—that was the
fourth day.

What do you think they painted?

_ _ _, _ _ _ _ _, _ _ _ _ _ _

The Hotshots were amazed at Kate's book of facts about the universe.

Check out some of these facts and amaze your friends with them.

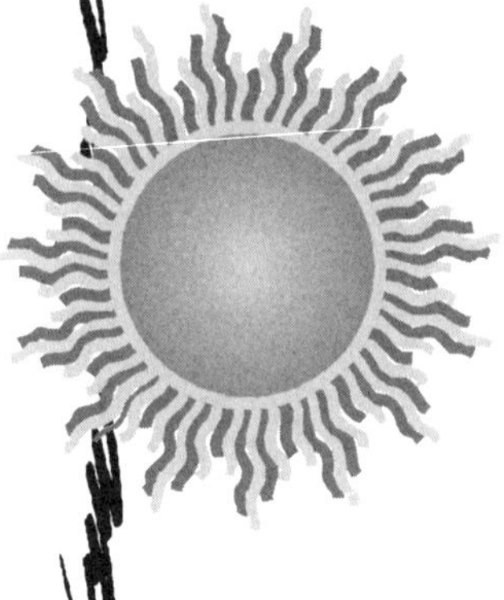

The sun is really a star. It is about 150 million kilometres away. We draw stars with points but they are really huge balls of burning gases. Light from the sun takes 8 minutes to reach the earth.

The light from the next nearest star takes four years.

The planets look like bright lights in the sky at night but they have no light at all. They are like the earth. We see them because they reflect light from the sun. There are at least 9 planets spinning around the sun. Most of them have moons. The earth only has one moon but Jupiter, the biggest planet has twelve moons.

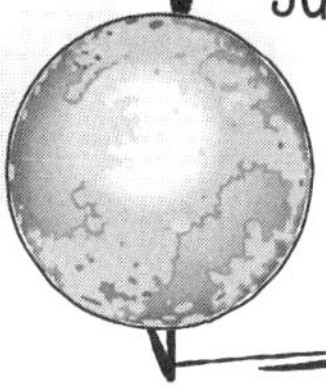

The closest planet to earth is Mars.
In 1996 the first spaceship was sent to Mars.
It took 7 months to get there.

Prayer:
Dear Lord, it's hard to understand the size of the universe you made. There's so much even the smartest people don't know about it. It makes me feel

______________________________.

5 Life in the air and sea

Reuben was outside the clubhouse waiting for the others. He moved a rock and it looked as if the ground underneath came to life! He saw beetles, a centipede, slaters, worms and lots of ants all scurrying to get away.

There was a time after God created the stars and planets when the earth and skies and seas came to life.

Genesis 1:20-23

[20] God said, "I command the ocean to be full
of living creatures, and I command birds to
fly above the earth." [21] So God made the
giant sea monsters and all the living
creatures that swim in the ocean. He also
made every kind of bird. God looked at what
he had done, and it was good. [22] Then he
gave the living creatures his blessing—he
told the ocean creatures to live everywhere
in the ocean and the birds to live
everywhere on earth. [23] Evening came and
then morning—that was the fifth day.

Prayer Idea:
Praise is when we tell God how great we think he is. We can sing our praise to God or say it or think or feel it. Praise God now in any way you like.

Something to do

Find a book about fish in the library. Which one do you think is most interesting? By the way, don't expect any book to tell you about all types of fish. There are more than 25,000!

DID YOU KNOW?

The biggest fish are 12 metres long but whales can be 30 metres.

The Blue Whale is thought to be the largest creature that ever lived. Just its tongue weighs 4 tons and is as big as an elephant.

Fish that live in the deepest part of the ocean where there's no light shine with their own light.

6 Life on earth

Genesis 1:24-25

24 God said, "I command the earth to give life to all kinds of tame animals, wild animals, and reptiles." And that's what happened. 25 God made every one of them. Then he looked at what he had done, and it was good.

There are so many different types of life on earth. Can you unjumble these letters to find some of them? The first letter of each word is underlined.

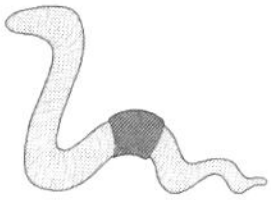

ntas, salinam,

____, _______,

bersliefutt, ssitnce,

______________, _______,

gorfs, romsw, ssderpi,

_____, _____, _______

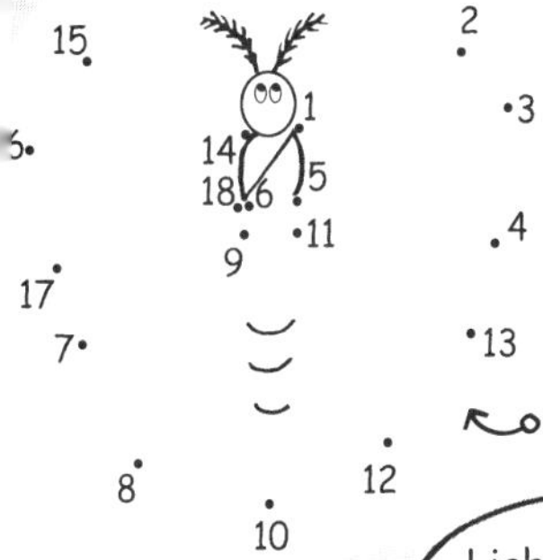

Join the dots to see one of these.

Prayer:
Thank you God for your wonderful world and all the different living things in it.

What a Dinosa

The word **'dinosaur'** means 'terrible lizard'.

There are no dinosaurs alive today. They all died out long ago, but their bones and footprints have been discovered in rocks all over the world. Scientists try to work out what dinosaurs looked like and what they did from their footprints and bones.

There were at least 5000 different kinds of dinosaurs. Here's just a few ...

Read on and see if you can find the answers to the Hotshots questions ...

…out …rs?

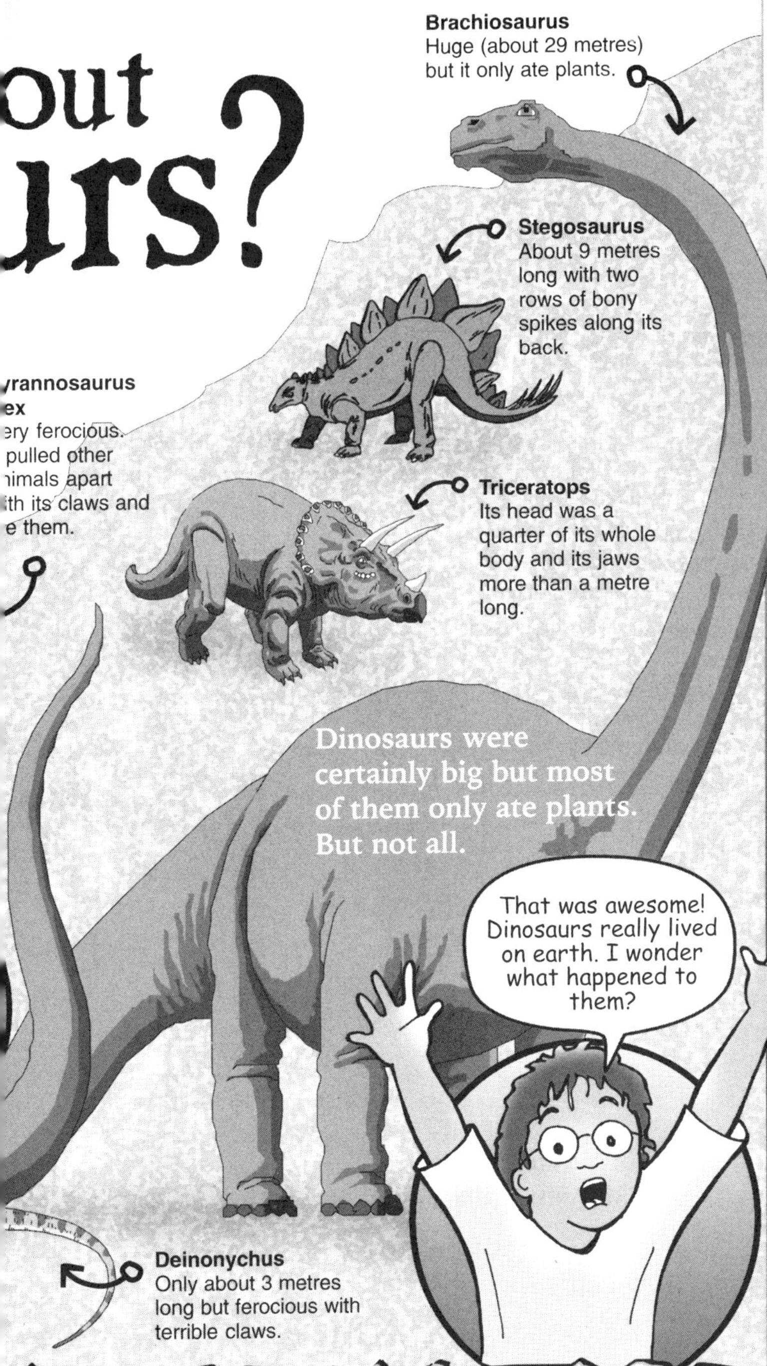

The Hotshots spotted these dinosaurs on their trip. See if you can work out which they are.

…here's a huge mystery about dinosaurs. Why did they all die out? Did new animals eat …ll their eggs? Did the climate change? Did meteorites hit them? No one really knows.

7 God saved the best till last

Back at the Clubhouse...

Genesis 1:26-31

26 God said, "Now we will make
humans, and they will be like us.
We will let them rule the fish, the
birds, and all other living creatures."

27 So God created humans to be like
himself; he made men and women.
28 God gave them his blessing and said:

Have a lot of children! Fill the earth
with people and bring it under your
control. Rule over the fish in the
ocean, the birds in the sky, and
every animal on the earth.

29 I have provided all kinds of fruit
and grain for you to eat. 30 And I
have given the green plants as food
for everything else that breathes.
These will be food for animals, both
wild and tame, and for birds.

31 God looked at what he had done. All
of it was very good! Evening came and
then morning—that was the sixth day.

Prayer:
Please God, help me to treat everything you've made with care. Help me to respect the world and live to make it a better place.

Then Kate told them something interesting.

'When God made the world he had a special job for people.'

God gave people the job of caring for his creation.

'Hey! That makes me one of God's park rangers!' grinned Reuben.

8 Microscopes and telescopes

God made billions of living creatures.

Some are so small you need a microscope to see them.

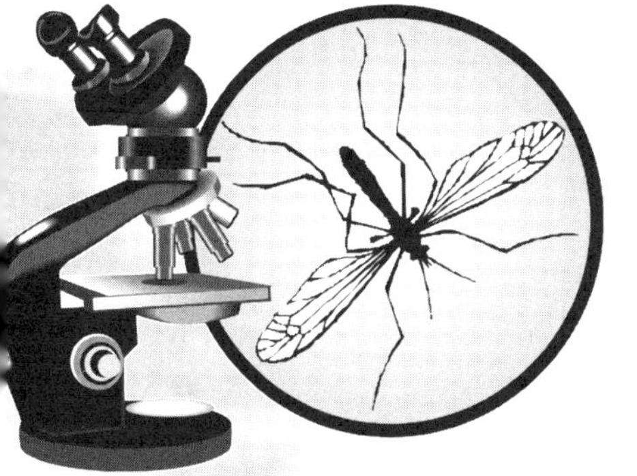

Can you think of 2 that are smaller than your thumb?

1. ....

2. ....

What about 2 that are more than twice the size of you?

1. ....

2. ....

Psalm 8:1,3-9

1 Our Lord and Ruler, your name is wonderful everywhere on earth!
You let your glory be seen in the heavens above.
3 I often think of the heavens your hands have made,
and of the moon and stars you put in place.
4 Then I ask, "Why do you care about us humans?
Why are you concerned for us weaklings?"
5 You made us a little lower than you yourself,
and you have crowned us with glory and honour.
6 You let us rule everything your hands have made.
And you put all of it under our power—
7 the sheep and the cattle, and every wild animal,
8 the birds in the sky, the fish in the sea, and all ocean creatures.
9 Our Lord and Ruler, your name is wonderful everywhere on earth!

We might seem weak beside some of these, but God made people SPECIAL.

Prayer idea:
How do you feel about having a special job to do for God? Talk to God about it. You might like to pray for help to do your very best for God.

Something to do

Can you find the Psalms in a Bible? Look about the middle. How many psalms are there? (__________)

9 Did it just happen?

Scientists like to find out what makes things happen. They know that things fall down because of a force called gravity. They know that puddles disappear because warmth from the sun turns the water into invisible gas.

How did the world happen?
(Use the code to check your answer.)

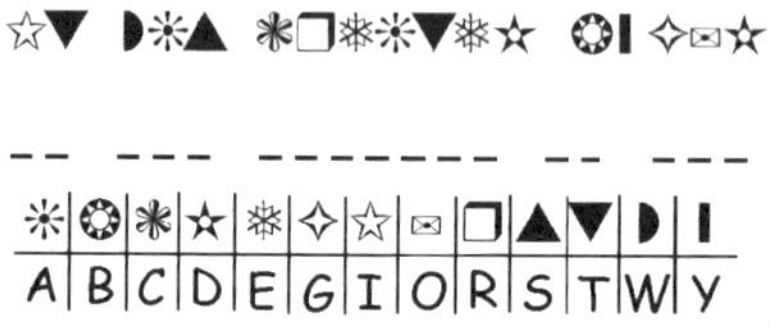

Scientists would like to know more about how God created. Perhaps one day they'll be able to tell us about the mysteries the Bible doesn't explain.

The Hotshots smiled as they looked at their creation mural. It was good and they felt pleased. How do you think God felt when he finished creating the world? The Bible tells us.

Genesis 2:1-4

So the heavens and the earth and everything else were created.

2 By the seventh day God had finished his work, and so he rested. 3 God blessed the seventh day and made it special because on that day he rested from his work.
4 That's how God created the heavens and the earth.

Prayer:
Thank you God for the good feeling we get when we've done something well. Please help me to do everything the best I can because I'm doing it for you.

Answers from page 11: banana, pine, tree, apricot, eggplant, cactus, palm, tomato, berries, rose, grass, ivy, fern nut

Creation mural

Here is a creation scene for you to colour in.

10 Warning!

The Hotshots were enjoying a snack together. There were grapes and strawberries but Alana was only eating grapes.

'I can't eat strawberries,' Alana told them. 'I'm allergic to them.'

'Can't eat strawberries?' asked Sean. 'That must be awful!'

'Not really,' said Alana. 'There's so many other good things to eat. And I don't want to get sick.'

It was like that for the man God made. There was just one thing he wasn't allowed to eat.

Genesis 2:15-17

15 The Lord God put the man in the
Garden of Eden to take care of it
and to look after it. 16 But the Lord
told him, "You may eat fruit from
any tree in the garden, 17 except the
one that has the power to let you
know the difference between right
and wrong. If you eat any fruit from
that tree, you will die before the
day is over!"

Why did the man need to leave the fruit from that tree alone?

Is there anything God might be warning you to leave alone?

Prayer idea:
Ask God to help you 'hear' what he's saying to you and help you do what he says.

Answer to the wordfind puzzle: God thought IT WAS GOOD

11 How the first woman was made

Genesis 2:18-25

18 The Lord God said, "It
isn't good for the man to live
alone. I need to make a suitable
partner for him." 19 So the
Lord took some soil and
made animals and birds. He
brought them to the man to
see what names he would give
each of them. Then the man
named the tame animals
and the birds and the
wild animals. That's
how they got their names.

None of these was the
right kind of partner for
the man. 21 So the Lord God
made him fall into a deep sleep,
and he took out one of the man's
ribs. Then after closing the
man's side, 22 the Lord made
a woman out of the rib.

The Lord God brought her to the
man, 23 and the man exclaimed,

"Here is someone like me!
She is part of my body,
my own flesh and bones.
She came from me, a man.
So I will name her Woman!"

24 That's why a man will
leave his own father and
mother. He marries a
woman, and the two of them
become like one person.

25 Although the man and his wife
were both naked, they were not
ashamed.

Do you ever have questions about the Bible?

What do you do when you have questions about the Bible? Is there an older person you know who reads their Bible? You could ask them. Your Mum or Dad might know, or you Sunday School or Kids Club leader. It's good to ask questions.

But it's better to look for answers!

Prayer:
Dear Lord, There's so much about the Bible I don't understand. Please help me to tune in to you as I read it so that you can tell me what you want me to know and do.

12 Disaster!

Everything was perfect in the garden.
Things couldn't be better UNTIL....

Genesis 3:1-7

The snake was sneakier than any
of the other wild animals that the
Lord God had made. One day it
came to the woman and asked,
"Did God tell you not to eat fruit
from any tree in the garden?"

2 The woman answered, "God said
we could eat fruit from any tree
in the garden, 3 except the one in
the middle. He told us not to eat
fruit from that tree or even to
touch it. If we do, we will die."

4 "No, you won't!" the snake
replied. 5 "God understands what
will happen on the day you eat
fruit from that tree.
You will see
what you have
done, and you
will know the
difference
between right
and wrong, just
as God does."

6 The woman stared at the fruit.
It looked beautiful and tasty. She
wanted the wisdom that it would
give her, and she ate some of the
fruit. Her husband was there with
her, so she gave some to him, and
he ate it too. 7 Right away they
saw what they had done, and they
realized they were naked. Then
they sewed fig leaves together
to make something to cover
themselves.

Prayer idea:
Is there something you feel bad about because it goes against what God wants? Tell God how you feel and what you want to do about it. God wants things between you and him to be perfect again.

13 Who's fault is it?

Today's Bible bit is something like that.

Genesis 3:8-13

8 Late in the afternoon a breeze began to blow, and the man and woman heard the Lord God walking in the garden. They were frightened and hid behind some trees.

9 The Lord called out to the man and asked, "Where are you?"

10 The man answered, "I was naked, and when I heard you walking through the garden, I was frightened and hid!"

11 "How did you know you were naked?" God asked. "Did you eat any fruit from that tree in the middle of the garden?"

12 "It was the woman you put here with me," the man said. "She gave me some of the fruit, and I ate it."

13 The Lord God then asked the woman, "What have you done?"

"The snake tricked me," she answered. "And I ate some of that fruit."

Prayer:
Dear God, you see me all the time. Please help me to do what will please you.

Quiz

1. Did the man and woman both try to hide?
   YES NO
2. Did the man try to blame someone else?
   YES NO
3. Did the woman try to blame someone else?
   YES NO
4. Have you ever tried to blame someone else when it was your fault?
   YES NO
5. Do you think we can ever hide from God?
   YES NO

Conseque

Join each outer oval with its consequences in the circles.

The mural was brilliant!

He's becoming a good guitar player.

She got big red bumps all over her.

He brok his arm

She knows a lot about God.

She was in trouble with her Mum.

The Hotshots worked hard on the mural.

Reuben fell from a tree.

Alana ate strawberries.

nces

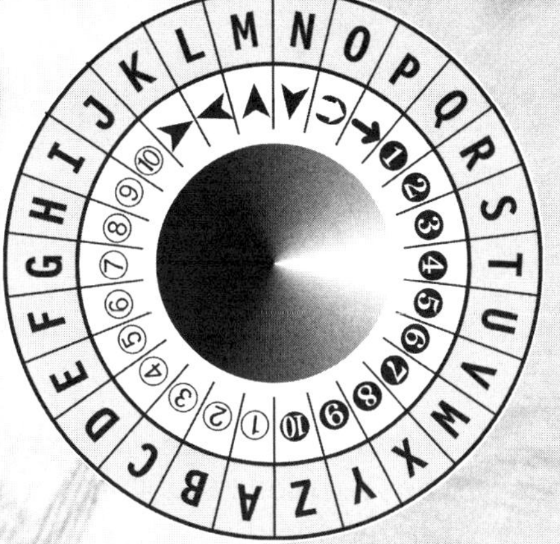

When the man and woman God made disobeyed him and ate the fruit, there were consequences too. The consequences were for them and everyone who came after them.

Use the code wheel to work out the consequences.

❹⑧⑤❾ ❼⊃❺◀④ ④⑨⑤

& They would die

❹⑧⑤❷⑤ ❼⊃❺◀④ ②⑤
❸❺⑥⑥⑤❷⑨▼⑦ ①▼④ ➔①⑨▼

⑦❷⊃❼⑨▼⑦ ⑥⊃⊃④ ❼⊃❺◀④
②⑤ ⑧①❷④ ❼⊃❷➤

⑥❷⑨⑤▼④❸⑧⑨➔ ❼⑨❹❽ ⑦⊃④
❼①❸ ❸➔⊃⑨◀❹

14 What happened after that?

Do you know the names of the man and woman we have been reading about?

Colour all the shapes with a cross one colour. Colour the shapes with a dot a different colour. Can you see their names?

They were the first to disobey in the wonderful world God made. Ever since, people have been doing things against God that upset others and spoil the world. The Bible calls that SIN.

Genesis 4:1-7

Adam and Eve had a son. Then Eve said,
"I'll name him Cain because I got him
with the help of the Lord." 2 Later she
had another son and named him Abel.

Abel became a sheep farmer, but Cain
farmed the land. 3 One day, Cain gave part
of his harvest to the Lord, 4 and Abel also
gave an offering to the Lord. He killed
the first-born lamb from one of his sheep
and gave the Lord the best parts of it.
The Lord was pleased with Abel and his
offering, 5 but not with Cain and his
offering. This made Cain so angry that
he could not hide his feelings.

6 The Lord said to Cain:

What's wrong with you? Why do you have
such an angry look on your face? 7 If you
had done the right thing, you would be
smiling. But you did the wrong thing, and
now sin is waiting to attack you like a lion.
Sin wants to destroy you, but don't let it!

Underline the warning God gave Cain.

Prayer:
Please God, help me to know when something is sin. Don't let sin destroy me.

CAN YOU FIND OUT

Did Cain listen to God? Find a Bible and look up Genesis 4:8.

YES / NO

15 From perfect to impossible

On the table in the clubhouse was a big glass of clean water. Kate had an eye dropper with black ink inside. The Hotshots watched as she let one drop fall into the glass.

'Who'd like a cool drink?' she smiled.

They looked as the black drop spread, turning the water a murky grey colour.

'Yuk! No thanks!'

'What if I put in more black?' asked Kate.

'No way! You've spoilt it now,' said Sean. 'It doesn't matter what you do it will still be horrible. You'll have to tip it out and start again.'

When God made the world everything was good. But because people disobeyed God, it didn't stay that way.

Genesis 6:5-7

5 The Lord saw how bad the people on
earth were and that everything they
thought and planned was evil. 6 He was
very sorry that he had made them,
7 and he said, "I'll destroy every living
creature on earth! I'll wipe out people,
animals, birds, and reptiles. I'm sorry
I ever made them."

Prayer idea:
God is sorry when people plan evil instead of good. Pray that people in the government will understand what is good and stand up against evil. Pray for yourself and people you know to do the same.

16 Good news bad news

Genesis 6:8-18

8 But the Lord was pleased
with Noah, 9 and this is the
story about him. Noah was
the only person who lived
right and obeyed God. 10 He
had three sons: Shem, Ham,
and Japheth.

11 God knew that everyone
was terribly cruel and
violent. 13 So he told Noah:

Cruelty and violence have
spread everywhere. Now
I'm going to destroy the
whole earth and all its
people. 14 Get some good
lumber and build a boat. Put
rooms in it and cover it with
tar inside and out. 15 Make
it four hundred fifty feet
long, seventy-five feet
wide, and forty-five feet
high. 16 Build a roof on the
boat and leave a space of
about eighteen inches
between the roof and the
sides. Make the boat three
stories high and put a door
on one side.

17 I'm going to send a flood
that will destroy everything
that breathes! Nothing will
be left alive. 18 But I
solemnly promise that you,
your wife, your sons, and
your daughters-in-law will
be kept safe in the boat.

When God decided to give the cruel, evil world a fresh start, it was good news for some people but bad news for everyone else.

How many people were going to be saved?

Prayer:
Thank you God that you won't put up with cruel and violent people forever. Thank you that you protect those who love good.

things to know

DID YOU KNOW that the boat God told Noah to build was big enough to fit 432 double decker buses? That was plenty of room for all the animals and Noah and his family.

17 Doing what God says

'I read the next part of the Noah story in my Bible last night,' said Reuben. There's one verse that could be a club motto for Hotshots.'

See if you can find it.

Genesis 6:18-22

18 But I solemnly promise that you,
your wife, your sons, and your
daughters-in-law will be kept safe
in the boat.

19 Bring into the boat with you a male
and a female of every kind of animal
and bird, as well as a male and a
female of every reptile. I don't want
them to be destroyed. 21 Store up
enough food both for yourself and
for them.

22 Noah did everything the Lord
told him to do.

'I like the last verse,' said Reuben, 'without the Noah bit.

Let's make our motto 'We do everything the Lord tells us to do!'

'But we don't always!' exclaimed Alana.

'But we try,' Suzy said.

In the end they decided on a motto everyone was happy with.

Prayer:
God, sometimes it's hard to know what you're saying to me. Sometimes I know but it's hard to do it. Please help me to know how important it is to do what you say.

Can you read it? Try holding it in front of a mirror.

18 Follow God's instructions

Prayer Idea:
Before the Hotshots read the next part of the Noah story they prayed that God would help them understand. Why don't you do the same?

Genesis 7:1-10

The Lord told Noah:

1 Take your whole family
with you into the boat,
because you are the only
one on this earth who
pleases me. 2 Take seven
pairs of every kind of
animal that can be used for
sacrifice and one pair of all
others. 3 Also take seven
pairs of every kind of bird
with you. Do this so there
will always be animals and
birds on the earth. 4 Seven
days from now I will send
rain that will last for forty
days and nights, and I will
destroy all other living
creatures I have made.

5 Noah was six hundred
years old when he went
into the boat to escape
the flood, and he did
everything the Lord had
told him to do. His wife, his
sons, and his daughters-in-
law all went inside with
him. 8 He obeyed God and
took a male and a female of
each kind of animal and
bird into the boat with him.
10 Seven days later a flood
began to cover the earth.

The Hotshots had questions:

Read verses 1 and 2 again and see of you can answer Mei and Suzy's questions.

19

Peace at last

Kate invited the Hotshots to a pizza and video night. In the movie a whole town was destroyed by a hurricane.

From Genesis 8

God did not forget about
Noah and the animals
with him in the
boat. So God
made a wind
blow, and the water
started going down.
3 For one hundred
fifty days the water slowly
went down. 4 Then ... the
boat came to rest
somewhere in the
Ararat mountains.

6 Forty days later Noah
opened a window to send
out a raven, but it kept
flying around until the
water had dried up.
8 Noah wanted to find
out if the water had
gone down, and he sent out a dove. 9 ... the
dove could not find a place to land. So it flew
back to the boat.

10 Seven days later Noah sent the dove out
again. 11 It returned in the evening, holding in
its beak a green leaf from an olive tree. Noah
knew that the water was finally going down.

15(Later) God said to Noah, 16 "You, your wife,
your sons, and your daughters-in-law may now
leave the boat. 17 Let out the birds, animals,
and reptiles, so they can mate and live all over
the earth." 18 After Noah and his family had
gone out of the boat, 19 the living creatures
left in groups of their own kind.

Prayer:
Thank you God that you don't forget those who love and obey you. Thank you that we are safe with you forever, even if the worst happens.

20 A fresh start

What do you think Noah said when he stepped out of the boat?

He didn't have to worry any more about being bashed on the head or protecting his family or property.

God had wiped out the evil. It was a new world.

Genesis 9:1, 8-11

God said to Noah and his sons:

1 I am giving you my blessing. Have a lot of children and grandchildren, so people will live everywhere on this earth.
8 Again, God said to Noah and his sons:

9 I am going to make a solemn promise to you and to everyone who will live after you.
10 This includes the birds and the animals that came out of the boat.
11 I promise every living creature that the earth and those living on it will never again be destroyed by a flood.

Why do you think God bothers with people? Why does he care what we do? God doesn't have to promise us anything. Why do you think he does?

Alana and Sean wrote their answers as puzzles. Can you work them out?

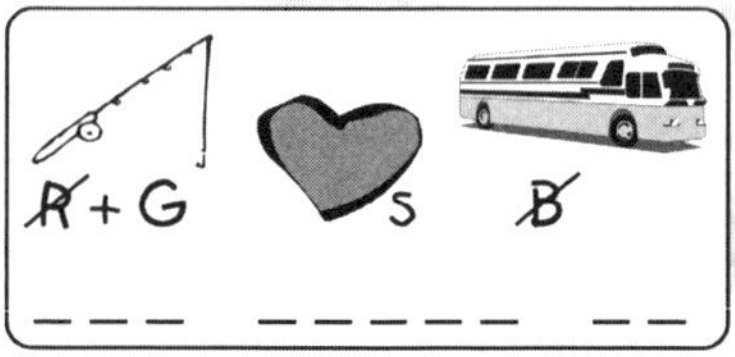

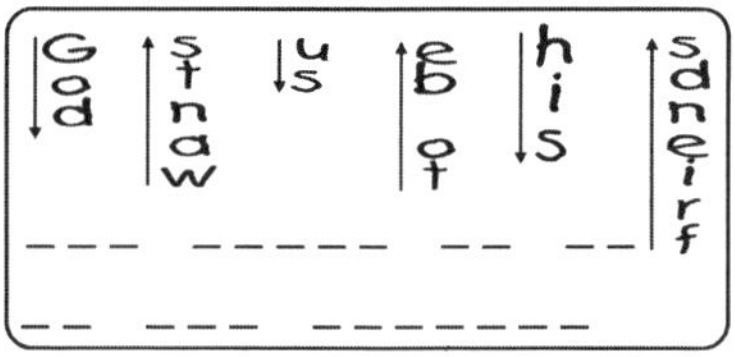

Prayer idea:
God has decided to always love you. What would you like to say to him?

21 Why are there different languages?

Genesis 11:1-9

At first everyone spoke
the same language, 2 but
after some of them moved
from the east and settled
in Babylonia, 3 they said:

4 Let's build a city with a
tower that reaches to the
sky! We'll use hard bricks
and tar instead of stone
and mortar. We'll become
famous, and we won't be
scattered all over the
world.

5 But when the Lord came
down to look at the city
and the tower, 6 he said:

These people are working
together because they all
speak the same language.
This is just the beginning.
Soon they will be able to
do anything they want.
7 Come on! Let's go down
and confuse them by
making them speak
different languages—
then they won't be able
to understand each other.

8 So the people had to
stop building the city,
because the Lord
confused their language
and scattered them all
over the earth. That's
how the city of Babel
got its name.

Do you remember what God told the survivors to do after the flood? Check out Genesis 9:1.

SPREADXOUTXALLXOVERXTHEXEARTH

What did they plan to do instead?

There's a hidden message on the bricks in the tower. Can you unjumble it?

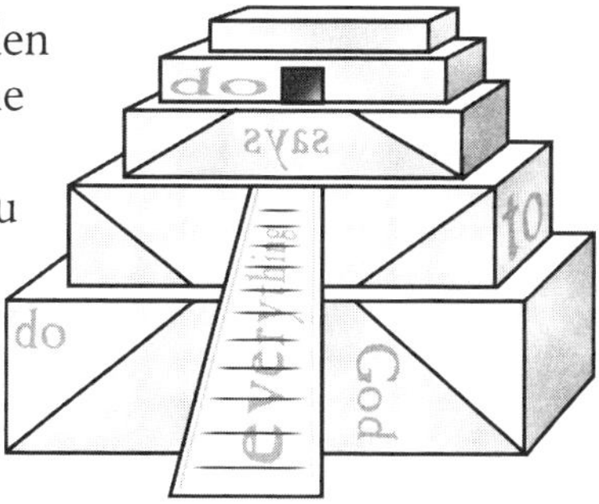

Prayer:
Lord, when I start to think my ideas are more important than yours, please remind me what you are like.

What do

There was a big question mark on the clubhouse door.

The Hotshots all wanted to know why it was there.

They noticed the bowls of nibblies inside!

you think?

'Aren't we going to read the Bible?' asked Mei.

'Maybe later,' answered Kate. 'But for now let's think about the Bible stories we've already read.'

They talked about the stories then painted words about God on a big sheet of paper. Then they stood back and looked at it.

'Yes,' Sean said.

'Sort of,' said Alana slowly. But maybe he's not so powerful now he's stopped creating.'

'But he did things after that. What about that huge flood and saving Noah?' answered Sean.

'And making the different languages?' added Mei.

'Maybe he's still like that but we don't notice so much,' said Sean.

'I reckon you're right!' Kate said. 'I'm going to try to notice what God is doing.'

Prayer idea: You might like to pray that God will help you notice what he's doing in the world now.

22 What's God doing?

The person who wrote this Psalm praised God for things God does everyday to care for his creation. Underline them as you find them. How many are there?

Psalm 104:1-20, 33

1 I praise you, Lord God,
with all my heart.
You are glorious and
majestic,
dressed in royal robes
2 and surrounded by light.
You spread out the sky
like a tent,
3 and you built your home
over the mighty ocean.
The clouds are your chariot
with the wind as its wings.
4 The winds are your
messengers,
and flames of fire
are your servants.
5 You built foundations
for the earth, and it
will never be shaken.
6 You covered the earth
with the ocean that rose
above the mountains.
7 Then your voice thundered!
And the water flowed
8 down the mountains
and through the valleys
to the place you prepared.
9 Now you have set boundaries,
so that the water will never
flood the earth again.

10 You provide streams of water
in the hills and valleys,
11 so that the donkeys
and other wild animals
can satisfy their thirst.
12 Birds build their nests nearby
and sing in the trees.
13 From your home above
you send rain on the hills
and water the earth.
14 You let the earth produce
grass for cattle,
plants for our food,
15 wine to cheer us up,
olive oil for our skin,
and grain for our health.
16 Our Lord, your trees
always have water,
and so do the cedars
you planted in Lebanon.
17 Birds nest in those trees,
and storks make their home
in the fir trees.
18 Wild goats find a home
in the tall mountains,
and small animals can hide
between the rocks.
19 You created the moon
to tell us the seasons.
The sun knows when to set,
20 and you made the darkness,
so the animals in the forest
could come out at night.
33 As long as I live,
I will sing and praise you,
the Lord God.

Prayer Idea:
Look at the first few verses again. You might like to say them as a prayer to God.

Finished...

but just beginnin

But God didn't give up on them. He promised that one day he would send someone special to make things right.
That person is Jesus.
On the cross Jesus said...
It's finished!
He did all he needed to do to make the world right again.
Jesus died to save everyone who wants to be free from sin and live with God forever.
But it's not right yet.
One day Jesus will come back and wipe out evil forever.
Those who are on his side will be saved and the whole world will be new, just like it was in the beginning.
Until then, God has a job for us. He wants us to show others what it's like to be on God's side. He wants us to live like Jesus lived, the way we will in the new world.
Impossible? It would be except for Jesus' special gift to his followers. You can find out about it in the coming pages ...

23 Wait!

The Hotshots were having a Scavenger Hunt.

As soon as he saw the lists of things to find, Sean grabbed one and raced off. He wanted to be the first to find everything.

'Wait!' Come back!' Kate called after him 'You can't do it without these.'

She handed everyone a pack with a map, collection bag and gloves.

Once Jesus gave his disciples a huge job to do. They had to tell everyone about Jesus – all over the world. But there was no point in starting until they had all they needed.

Prayer idea:
Dear Lord, Sometimes it's really hard to do what you want. I especially need your help to ________________

____

(add what you need help with). Thank you for giving the Holy Spirit to help me do what your want.

Acts 1:3-5

3 For forty days after Jesus had suffered and died, he proved in many ways that he had been raised from death. He appeared to his apostles and spoke to them about God's kingdom. 4 While he was still with them, he said:

Don't leave Jerusalem yet. Wait here for the Father to give you the Holy Spirit, just as I told you he has promised to do. 5 John baptized with water, but in a few days you will be baptized with the Holy Spirit.

Colour the shapes with a dot to see why they had to wait.

hotshots help *you* to read and understand the Bible

HOT new series

The first four books are about a Basketball Club:

- **The World's Greatest Leader – ever!**
- **Mini-Stars of the Bible**
- **Growing as a Follower of Jesus**
- **Sticking Close to God**

Then there are more Hotshots books …

These books feature a new Kids' Club, their leader Kate, and their very own **Time Machine!**

Keep reading the Hotshots series – they will help you read the Bible.

Kate invited Alana's Aunty Rina to the clubhouse to show the Hotshots her photos.

MOUNT

'You went there?' asked Reuben. 'How?'

'I took a plane to Jerusalem.' she said.

'Like this!' said Rina pointing to the photo. 'It's rocky. There were lots of churches.'

'How should I know?' Rina laughed. 'I only know what it was like last year!'

All the Hotshots were thinking about the time-ship. *That's* how they could find out what Mount Olive was like when Jesus was there. As soon as Aunty Rina left everyone said together...

Two thousand years ago there were no churches on the mountain slope only lots of olive trees and a path leading down into Jerusalem. For thousands of years people have walked on this mountain slope outside Jerusalem. People still do today.

24 God's way of being with us

Acts 1:6-11

6 While the apostles were
still with Jesus, they asked
him, "Lord, are you now going to
give Israel its own king again?"

7 Jesus said to them, "You don't need to
know the time of those events that only
the Father controls. 8 But the Holy
Spirit will come upon you and give you
power. Then you will tell everyone about
me in Jerusalem, in all Judea, in
Samaria, and everywhere in the world."
9 After Jesus had said this and while
they were watching, he was taken up
into a cloud. They could not see him,
10 but as he went up, they kept looking
up into the sky.

Suddenly two men dressed in white
clothes were standing there beside
them. 11 They said, "Why are you men
from Galilee standing here and looking
up into the sky? Jesus has been taken
to heaven. But he will come back in the
same way that you have seen him go."

The disciples could see God's power by watching Jesus when he was with them.

1. *When Jesus went back to heaven, who would have that power? (verse 8)*

   ____

   ____

2. *Where would they get it?*

   ____

   ____

Prayer:
Lord God, please teach me more about your Holy Spirit. Most of all, make me pleased to welcome your Spirit into my life every day.

Do you have a question about the Holy Spirit? Go to someone who loves God and see if they can answer you.

Answers: 1.The disciples 2.The Holy Spirit.

25 Being with Jesus

Jesus chose 12 disciples to be with him. Do you know the full name of the one who was a traitor?

Write the first letter of each picture to spell his name.
Judas wasn't around after Jesus went back to heaven.

Find out what sort of person the disciples were looking for to take the place of this Judas.

To tell others about Jesus we need to spend time with him so we really know him.

Talk to him whenever you think of him during the day. He's right there with you by his Holy Spirit.

Acts 1:12-13, 21-22

12 The Mount of Olives was about half a mile from Jerusalem. The apostles who had gone there were Peter, John, James, Andrew, Philip, Thomas, Bartholomew, Matthew, James the son of Alphaeus, Simon, known as the Eager One, and Judas the son of James.

After the apostles returned to the city, they went upstairs to the room where they had been staying.

21-22 "We need someone else to help us tell others that Jesus has been raised from death. He must also be one of the men who was with us from the very beginning. He must have been with us from the time the Lord Jesus was baptized by John until the time he was taken to heaven."

Prayer idea:
Why don't you take a bit longer praying today? You could make a list of some things that are important to you at the moment. Then talk to God about them. The more you share with him, the better friends you'll become.

26 Choosing

How is your school captain chosen?

- ❑ everyone votes
- ❑ the teachers decide
- ❑ someone draws a name from a hat

How do you think the disciples chose the new disciple?

Read Acts 1: 23-26

23 Two men were
suggested: One of them
was Joseph Barsabbas,
known as Justus, and the
other was Matthias.
24 Then they all prayed,
"Lord, you know what
everyone is like! Show us
the one you have chosen
25 to be an apostle and to
serve in place of Judas,
who got what he
deserved." 26 They drew
names, and Matthias was
chosen to join the group
of the eleven apostles.

Put the steps in the order they did them.

THINK

◯ ◯ ◯

CHOOSE PRAY

Prayer:
Lord God, Thank you for wanting to be involved in everything I do. Please help me to be wise and choose what's best.

27 Power from God

Jesus promised them POWER.

Read what it was like.

Acts 2:1-4

On the day of
Pentecost all the
Lord's followers were
together in one place.
2 Suddenly there was
a noise from heaven
like the sound of a
mighty wind! It filled
the house where they
were meeting. 3 Then
they saw what looked
like fiery tongues
moving in all
directions, and a
tongue came and
settled on each
person there.
4 The Holy Spirit took
control of everyone,
and they began
speaking whatever
languages the Spirit
let them speak.

If you were waiting there with the disciples what would you see?

What would you hear?

What would you feel?

You might like to read the Bible bit again imaging you are there.

What would you tell your friends about the Holy Spirit after that?

In the box, draw or write about what happened.

Prayer:
God, when I think about your Holy Spirit

I feel ____________________

I wish ____________________

I'm glad that ____________________

Please help me to ____________________

28 God stirs things up

Mei held out a tiny greenish bundle. 'It was a grub yesterday and now look at it! God's going to turn it into a butterfly. I know he is!'

'Good spotting, Mei,' grinned Reuben.

But Alana was quiet. 'God's not doing that. It just happens,' she said.

When amazing things happened in Jerusalem some people didn't think it was anything special at all.

Prayer:
Great and powerful God. You are at work in this world all the time. Please help all your people to see what you are doing. Help us to help others see too.

Acts 2:5-13

5 Many religious Jews from every
country in the world were living in
Jerusalem. 6 And when they heard
this noise, a crowd gathered. But
they were surprised, because they
were hearing everything in their own
languages. 7 They were excited and
amazed, and said:

Don't all these who are speaking
come from Galilee? 8 Then why do
we hear them speaking our very own
languages? 9 Some of us are from
Parthia, Media, and Elam. Others
are from Mesopotamia, Judea,
Cappadocia, Pontus, Asia, 10 Phrygia,
Pamphylia, Egypt, parts of Libya near
Cyrene, Rome, 11 Crete, and Arabia.
Some of us were born Jews, and
others of us have chosen to be Jews.
Yet we all hear them using our own
languages to tell the wonderful things
God has done.

12 Everyone was excited and confused.
Some of them even kept asking each
other, "What does all this mean?"

13 Others made fun of the Lord's
followers and said, "They are drunk."

Three in One

Kevin Keen lives next door to the clubhouse.

He's a smart friendly neighbour who gives the Hotshots a cheery wave when he sees them.

'Hello, Mr Keen.' They call out to him.

Billy Keen is only three. When Mr Keen comes home from work Billy runs to him and calls out 'Daddy!'

Sometimes Kevin Keen's mother comes to stay next door. She's Billy's grandma. Mr Keen picks her up at the station and carries her bags. When she gets off the train she calls out 'Kevin!'

Mr Keen, Daddy, Kevin.
Three people in one.

Have you ever heard of the word 'Trinity'?

It's not in the Bible but it's a word about God. It means three in one.

There is only one true God.

The Father, the Son and The Holy Spirit are all the one true God.

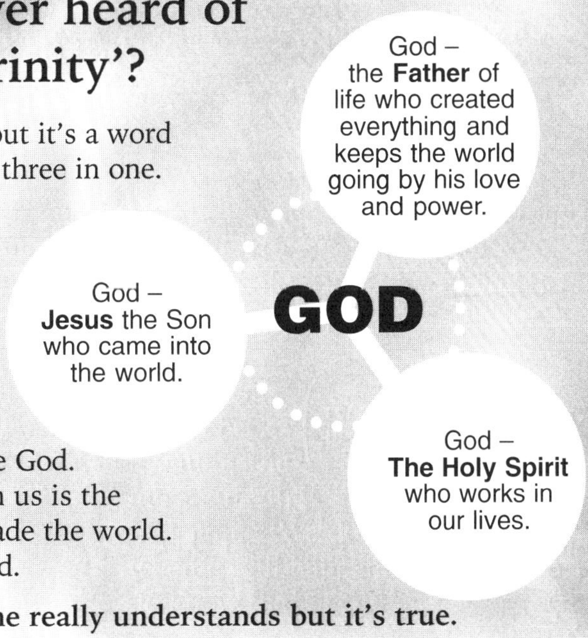

There's only one true God. The God who lives in us is the same as God who made the world. Jesus is the same God.

It's a mystery no one really understands but it's true.

29 A Riddle

'He made a perfect world, then he destroyed it?' suggested Mei.

'He flooded the earth and then dried it up? said Suzy.

'No. I'll give you a clue. It's about languages.'

'I'm confused!' said Suzy.

Acts 2:14-18

14 Peter stood with the eleven
apostles and spoke in a loud and
clear voice to the crowd:

Friends and everyone else living
in Jerusalem, listen carefully to
what I have to say! 15 You are
wrong to think that these
people are drunk. After all, it is
only nine o'clock in the morning.
16 But this is what God had the
prophet Joel say,

17 "When the last days come,
I will give my Spirit
to everyone.
Your sons and daughters
will prophesy.
Your young men
will see visions,
and your old men
will have dreams.
18 In those days I will give
my Spirit to my servants,
both men and women,
and they will prophesy.

The coming of the Holy Spirit was part of what God planned long before. It was another step towards God's new world.

If you give up on Sean's riddle like the other Hotshots you can find the answer on page 63.

Prayer:
Thank you God that you are working out your plans. Thank you that your Spirit is for everyone. And thank you for

___

30 The most important thing

What is the most important thing in the world?

When Peter started preaching, the most important thing in the world to him was a person. Who?

Acts 2:22-24

22 Now, listen to what I have to say about Jesus from Nazareth. God proved that he sent Jesus to you by having him work miracles, wonders, and signs. All of you know this. 23 God had already planned and decided that Jesus would be handed over to you. So you took him and had evil men put him to death on a cross. 24 But God set him free from death and raised him to life. Death could not hold him in its power.

Underline something very important things about Jesus in the Bible bit.

Prayer:
Take a minute to think about Jesus and how important he is to you. Tell him now by praying.

31 Turn back to God

Prayer idea:
How do you feel when you think about Jesus dying to save you? Before you read any more you might like to tell God how you feel.

Peter must have been glad that Jesus died to save him, but he was worried about others. He wanted them to be saved too.

Acts 2:37-41

37 When the people
heard this, they were
very upset. They asked
Peter and the other
apostles, "Friends,
what shall we do?"

38 Peter said, "Turn
back to God! Be
baptized in the name
of Jesus Christ, so
that your sins will be
forgiven. Then you
will be given the Holy
Spirit. 39 This promise
is for you and your
children. It is for
everyone our Lord God
will choose, no matter
where they live."

40 Peter told them
many other things as
well. Then he said,
"I beg you to save
yourselves from what
will happen to all these
evil people." 41 On
that day about three
thousand believed his
message and were
baptized.

Write in the bubble what you think is the important part of what Peter said.

Do you know people who need to turn back to God to be saved? Pray for them now.

Prayer:
Dear God, you want everyone to be saved and be part of the new world you will make one day.
I pray for ____________________

and ____________________

Please help them to turn to you.

32 A happy family

What makes a happy family?

All families are different. Tick the things your family likes to do together.

- [ ] Watch sport
- [ ] go to church
- [ ] play games
- [ ] go swimming
- [ ] pray
- [ ] ride bikes
- [ ] have dinner

The Bible says when the Holy Spirit came to Jesus' followers they were 'like family'. That was the church when it first began.

Acts 2:42-47

42 They spent their time learning from the
apostles, and they were like family to each
other. They also broke bread and prayed
together.

43 Everyone was amazed by the many miracles
and wonders that the apostles worked. 44 All
the Lord's followers often met together, and
they shared everything they had. 45 They
would sell their property and possessions and
give the money to whoever needed it. 46 Day
after day they met together in the temple.
They broke bread together in different
homes and shared their food happily and
freely, 47 while praising God. Everyone liked
them, and each day the Lord added to their
group others who were being saved.

Prayer idea:
There are those who follow Jesus in every country.
Pray for your 'brothers and sisters' all over the world.

33 Jesus heals again

Acts 3:1-10

The time of prayer was about three o'clock in the afternoon, and Peter and John were going into the temple. 2 A man who had been born lame was being carried to the temple door. Each day he was placed beside this door, known as the Beautiful Gate. He sat there and begged from the people who were going in.

3 The man saw Peter and John entering the temple, and he asked them for money. 4 But they looked straight at him and said, "Look up at us!"

5 The man stared at them and thought he was going to get something. 6 But Peter said, "I don't have any silver or gold! But I will give you what I do have. In the name of Jesus Christ from Nazareth, get up and start walking." 7 Peter then took him by the right hand and helped him up.

At once the man's feet and ankles became strong, 8 and he jumped up and started walking. He went with Peter and John into the temple, walking and jumping and praising God. 9 Everyone saw him walking around and praising God. 10 They knew that he was the beggar who had been lying beside the Beautiful Gate, and they were completely surprised. They could not imagine what had happened to the man.

After Jesus returned to heaven the Holy Spirit came to his followers. It was the Holy Spirit living in them that helped them do the sort of things Jesus did. That's been the job of the church ever since.

The Hotshots talked about what Jesus might want to do in their neighbourhood. They thought of things that weren't right and made a list.

What do you think God would like to happen in your home? In your school? In your neighbourhood?

Make your list here. Talk to someone else who you think would like to help put things right.

'Do you think God could use us to change some of those things?' asked Suzy.

'With the Holy Spirit in us we can do anything God wants us to!' replied Kate.

'Why don't we see if we can walk that big dog?'
'Or clean up the papers in the park!'

Prayer Idea:
Invite the Holy Spirit to use you to do what God wants.

34 Who did it?

'So who healed that man we read about last time?' asked Alana

'It was Peter wasn't it? Or was it John? One of them anyway,' answered Suzy.

'Think again!' said Kate. 'Let's not miss the most important part.'

They read the story again, then the part that answered Alana's question.

Read Acts 3:16

16 You see this man, and you know him. He put his faith in the name of Jesus and was made strong. Faith in Jesus made this man completely well while everyone was watching.

Who healed the man?

J	O	E
O	S	O
U	O	S

Cross out the 'O's

'But Jesus wasn't there! He already went back to heaven,' said Alana

'Peter and John had the Holy Spirit in them. The Holy Spirit is God, just like Jesus,' explained Suzy.

'WOW!' said Alana.

What was Alana thinking? Write it in the bubble.

Prayer:
Dear God I just want to tell you

that I think you're ______________

Please help me to ______________

35 Saving the world

Have you ever seen a movie in which someone saved the world?

Acts 4:1-16 selections

The apostles were still talking to the people, when some priests, the captain of the temple guard, and some Sadducees arrived. 3 It was already late in the afternoon, and they arrested Peter and John and put them in jail for the night. 4 But a lot of people who had heard the message believed it. So by now there were about five thousand followers of the Lord.

8 Peter was filled with the Holy Spirit and told the nation's leaders and the elders:

12 Only Jesus has the power to save! His name is the only one in all the world that can save anyone.

13 The officials were amazed to see how brave Peter and John were, and they knew that these two apostles were only ordinary men and not well educated. The officials were certain that these men had been with Jesus. 14 But they could not deny what had happened. The man who had been healed was standing there with the apostles.

15 The officials commanded them to leave the council room. Then the officials said to each other, 16 "What can we do with these men? Everyone in Jerusalem knows about this miracle, and we cannot say it didn't happen.

Sean saw one about a meteor crashing through space towards the earth. A space scientist blasted it and everything was OK.

In today's Bible bit Peter was in trouble for teaching about Jesus. He talked about saving the world.

Underline the words about Jesus saving the world. That's why Jesus is called the SAVIOUR.

Even if the whole earth is destroyed, Jesus' followers are safe with him. To be truly safe, everyone needs Jesus.

Prayer:
Lord Jesus, I'm glad you can save anyone who turns to you. Please help me to trust you always.

Have you ever asked Jesus to be your Saviour?
To find out more, turn to page 94.

36 The story continues...

Acts 4:5,7-10

5 The next morning the
leaders, the elders, and
the teachers of the Law
of Moses met in Jerusalem.
7 They brought in Peter and
John and made them stand
in the middle while they
questioned them. They
asked, "By what power and
in whose name have you
done this?"

8 Peter was filled with the
Holy Spirit and told the
nation's leaders and the
elders:

9 You are questioning us
today about a kind deed in
which a crippled man was
healed. 10 But there is
something we must tell you
and everyone else in Israel.
This man is standing here
completely well because of
the power of Jesus Christ
from Nazareth. You put
Jesus to death on a cross,
but God raised him to life.

The people at the start of the Bible story are the ones who had Jesus killed. How do you think they felt when they heard that Jesus was still doing things in their city? *Circle the right one/s.*

Do you think Peter and John were scared when they heard they had to go to the leaders?

☐ YES ☐ NO

Underline the words that tell where Peter got the power to tell them that Jesus was alive.

Prayer:
Is there something you know God wants you to do for him. Pray now that you'll have the power you need to do it well.

37 and continues...

God does great things with ordinary people. It's all part of his plan.

Can you think of any 'little' people in the Bible who did 'big' things for God?

Here are a few. Can you remember what they did? (If not ask someone who reads the Bible a lot.)

Acts 4:13-18

13 The officials were amazed to see
how brave Peter and John were, and
they knew that these two apostles
were only ordinary men and not well
educated. The officials were certain
that these men had been with Jesus.
14 But they could not deny what had
happened. The man who had been
healed was standing there with the
apostles.

15 The officials commanded them to
leave the council room. Then the
officials said to each other, 16 "What
can we do with these men? Everyone
in Jerusalem knows about this miracle,
and we cannot say it didn't happen.
17 But to keep this thing from
spreading, we will warn them never
again to speak to anyone about the
name of Jesus." 18 So they called the
two apostles back in and told them that
they must never, for any reason, teach
anything about the name of Jesus.

Peter and **John** were ordinary fishermen but see how brave they were!

God has great things for you to do too. If you're brave enough, pray this prayer!

Prayer:
Most Powerful God,
Fill me with your
Holy Spirit so that
nothing stops me
doing what you want
me to do all my life.

38 Did they obey?

Before Sean went to the Sports Carnival his Dad told him, 'Make sure you put on sunscreen every two hours.'

At the ground Sean left his bag where he was told and went to sit near the track with his class.

After 2 hours Sean remembered the sunscreen. He went to ask the teacher if he could go to his bag but as soon as he stood up the teacher called, 'Sean, sit down. The people behind can't see.'

Five minutes later he tried again but the same thing happened. He didn't know what to do.

Should he obey Dad or his teacher?

The apostles (disciples) faced a problem like that.

Who told them to tell everyone about Jesus? *(Tick)*

☐ Their dad, ☐ the king, ☐ Jesus

Who ordered them not to speak about Jesus?

☐ The CIA, ☐ the officials, ☐ their wives

Who do you think they obeyed?

____

Did they obey? continued ...

Now read the Bible bit to check your answer.

Acts 4: 19-23

19 Peter and John answered, "Do
you think God wants us to obey
you or to obey him? 20 We can't
keep quiet about what we've seen
and heard."

21-22 The officials couldn't find
any reason to punish Peter and
John. So they threatened them
and let them go. The man who
was healed by this miracle was
more than 40 years old, and
everyone was praising God for
what had happened.

23 As soon as Peter and John had
been set free, they went back
and told the others everything
that the chief priests and the
leaders had said to them.

things to know

Bible Discovery

One of Jesus' followers was called Barnabas. Find out what his name means in a Bible, Acts 4:36.

Why do you think Peter and John chose to obey Jesus instead of the officials?

Prayer:
Please God, Make me brave enough to do what you want even when others don't want me to.

Answer to the riddle on page 50: At Babel God made languages so people couldn't understand each other. At Pentecost he made his followers speak languages everyone could understand.

39 God knows everything

Have you ever said something that's not exactly true, to impress others?

That's what the Bible story is about. Read it now.

Acts 5:1-11

Ananias and his wife Sapphira also sold a piece of property. 2 But they agreed to cheat and keep some of the money for themselves.

So when Ananias took the rest of the money to the apostles, 3 Peter said, "Why has Satan made you keep back some of the money from the sale of the property? Why have you lied to the Holy Spirit? 4 The property was yours before you sold it, and even after you sold it, the money was still yours. What made you do such a thing? You didn't lie to people. You lied to God!"

5 As soon as Ananias heard this, he dropped dead, and everyone who heard about it was frightened. 6 Some young men came in and wrapped up his body. Then they took it out and buried it.

7 Three hours later Sapphira came in, but she did not know what had happened to her husband. 8 Peter asked her, "Tell me, did you sell the property for this amount?"

"Yes," she answered, "that's the amount."

9 Then Peter said, "Why did the two of you agree to test the Lord's Spirit? The men who buried Ananias are by the door, and they will carry you out!" 10 At once she fell at Peter's feet and died.

When the young men came back in, they found Sapphira lying there dead. So they carried her out and buried her beside her husband. 11 The church members were afraid, and so was everyone else who heard what had happened.

'What do you think about that?' said Kate.

Here's what the Hotshots said.

Did they obey? continued ...

Then they wanted to know what Kate thought.

Do you agree with Mei, Suzy, Alana, Reuben, Sean or Kate?

In the circles tick one or more that think like you. There's no one right answer.

Prayer idea:
Tell God how you honestly feel about what he did in today's Bible story. Ask him to teach you more about what he's really like.

40 How many Christians?

Kate had a magazine about Christians in other countries.

'Millions!' said Kate. 'Since Jesus went back to heaven, his followers have done the job Jesus gave them. The church is still growing. Remember we've got brothers and sisters all over the world.'

☐ How many people joined God's family the first time Peter preached? (Page 54)

☐ How many were there after the lame man was healed? (Page 59)

And that was just the start!

Acts 5:12-14

12 The apostles worked many miracles and wonders among the people. All of the Lord's followers often met in the part of the temple known as Solomon's Porch. 13 No one outside their group dared join them, even though everyone liked them very much.

14 Many men and women started having faith in the Lord.

Do you remember what they did when they met together? Acts 2:42-47 will remind you. Here's just a few things.

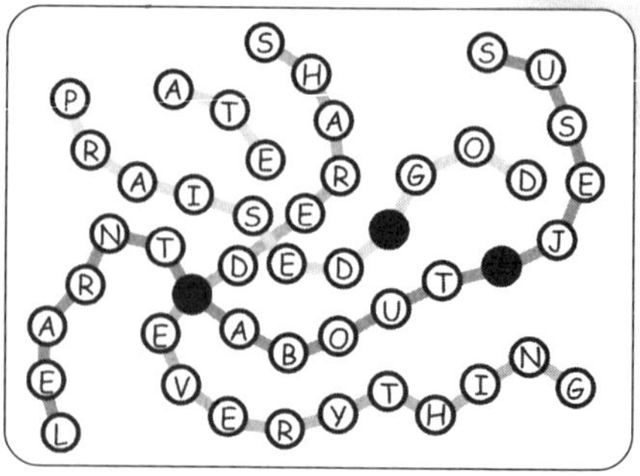

Prayer:
Heavenly Father, thanks that you are still working out your plan for a new world. It's great that more and more people are going to be part of it. Please help me to do my bit.

41

Saved for a reason

Have you ever been having so much fun you thought nothing could possibly go wrong?

Jesus' followers were excited about their life. God was working miracles with them. Everyone liked them and new people believed in Jesus and joined the church every day. But the leaders who caused trouble for them hadn't given up.

Read Acts 5:17-21

17 The high priest and all
the other Sadducees who
were with him became
jealous. 18 They arrested
the apostles and put them
in the city jail. 19 But that
night an angel from the
Lord opened the doors
of the jail and led the
apostles out. The angel
said, 20 "Go to the temple
and tell the people
everything about this new
life." 21 So they went into
the temple before sunrise
and started teaching.

The high priest and his men called together their council, which included all of Israel's leaders. Then they ordered the apostles to be brought to them from the jail.

Put a cross over the bad thing that happened. Put a tick over the good thing that happened.

Why did the angel let them out of jail?

Underline the angel's words.

God still had a job for the apostles to do. What was it?

That job's not over until Jesus returns.

TELLEVERYONEABOUTTHENEWLIFEJESUSGIVES

Prayer:
Thank you God that you help us do the job you gave us. Please help me to trust you even when it's hard.

42 Tricked!

Suzy found a lizard with a green stripe down its back. She carefully put it in a box to show the others. She put some dirt and grass in the box and some rocks for it to hide under. 'My lizard is so beautiful,' she told the Hotshots. But when they came to see it there was no lizard! It must have escaped, but Suzy had no idea how.

Acts 5:21-26

21 They went into the temple before sunrise and started teaching.

The high priest and his men called together their council, which included all of Israel's leaders. Then they ordered the apostles to be brought to them from the jail. 22 The temple police who were sent to the jail did not find the apostles. They returned and said, 23 "We found the jail locked tight and the guards standing at the doors. But when we opened the doors and went in, we didn't find anyone there." 24 The captain of the temple police and the chief priests listened to their report, but they did not know what to think about it.

25 Just then someone came in and said, "Right now those men you put in jail are in the temple, teaching the people!" 26 The captain went with some of the temple police and brought the apostles back. But they did not use force. They were afraid that the people might start throwing stones at them.

What a mystery! The most important people in the country were waiting for the apostles but they had escaped from inside a locked jail.

How did they get out?

____

Where were they?

____

What were they doing?

____

Prayer idea:
Thank you God for using your great power to help your people make good things happen.

43 Obey or not?

Acts 5:27-29

27 When the apostles were brought before the council, the high priest said to them, 28 "We told you plainly not to teach in the name of Jesus. But look what you have done! You have been teaching all over Jerusalem, and you are trying to blame us for his death."

29 Peter and the apostles replied:

We don't obey people. We obey God.

S	H	O	E	
G	S	U	N	
O	B	E	Y	
D	H	A	T	

Underline what Peter and the other apostles said.

'It depends on the people!' said Reuben quickly. 'Those leaders were the ones who had Jesus killed!'

'Don't obey people who are telling you to disobey God!' added Sean.

'Good thinking guys!' smiled Kate.

Black out the words of the pictures to see a hidden message.

Prayer:
Please God, give me courage to obey you at all times.
Help me to obey others when it is right.

44 You can't stop God

One of the leaders was a very wise man. Write the first letter of each picture to find his name. Underline it in the Bible bit.

____ ____ ____ ____ ____ ____ ____ ____

Read Acts 5:33-39

33 When the council members heard
this, they became so angry that they
wanted to kill the apostles. 34 But one
of the members was the Pharisee
Gamaliel, a highly respected teacher.
He ordered the apostles to be taken
out of the room for a little while.
35 Then he said to the council:

Be careful what you do with these
men. 36 Not long ago Theudas
claimed to be someone
important, and about four
hundred men joined him.
But he was killed. All his
followers were scattered,
and that was the end of that.

37 Later, when the people of our
nation were being counted, Judas
from Galilee showed up. A lot
of people followed him,
but he was killed, and all
his followers were
scattered.

38 So I advise you to stay
away from these men. Leave them
alone. If what they are planning is
something of their own doing, it
will fail. 39 But if God is behind it,
you cannot stop it anyway, unless
you want to fight against God.

The council members agreed with what he said.

Did the message about Jesus die out? No way! It's all part of God's great plan. People who love Jesus have been telling the message for nearly 2000 years and will keep telling it. The church will keep growing until Jesus comes back.

Prayer:
God, you are so powerful. No one and nothing can stop your plans. It's good to belong to you. It makes me feel

____

45 They never stopped

Reuben was very excited. He was going to visit his cousins who lived on an island.

Acts 5:40-42

40 and they called the apostles
back in. They had them beaten
with a whip and warned them
not to speak in the name of
Jesus. Then they let them go.

41 The apostles left the council
and were happy, because God
had considered them worthy
to suffer for the sake of
Jesus. 42 Every day they spent
time in the temple and in one
home after another. They
never stopped teaching and
telling the good news that
Jesus is the Messiah.

Reuben's visit was 6 months away but he never stopped talking about it. It didn't even bother him when he realised he would be away for the Show. 'Nothing's as good as what I'll be doing,' he kept saying.

The apostles were like that about Jesus. They didn't stop talking about him. They were even glad when others bashed them up for talking about Jesus.

Prayer:
How are you going with living for Jesus? Are you especially glad for something God has done recently? Do you need his help for something you want to do for him soon? Talk to him about it now.

46 Different jobs for different people

Acts 6:1-7

A lot of people were now becoming followers of the Lord. But some of the ones who spoke Greek started complaining about the ones who spoke Aramaic. They complained that the Greek-speaking widows were not given their share when the food supplies were handed out each day.

2 The twelve apostles called the whole group of followers together and said, "We should not give up preaching God's message in order to serve at tables.
3 My friends, choose seven men who are respected and wise and filled with God's Spirit. We will put them in charge of these things. 4 We can spend our time praying and serving God by preaching."

5 This suggestion pleased everyone, and they began by choosing Stephen. He had great faith and was filled with the Holy Spirit. Then they chose Philip, Prochorus, Nicanor, Timon, Parmenas, and also Nicolaus, who worshiped with the Jewish people in Antioch. 6 These men were brought to the apostles. Then the apostles prayed and placed their hands on the men to show that they had been chosen to do this work.
7 God's message spread, and many more people in Jerusalem became followers. Even a large number of priests put their faith in the Lord.

Circle the words that show not everyone was happy in the early church.

Underline the bit that tells what they did to solve the problem.

It's not everyone's job to preach and pray a lot. What were Stephen and the others chosen to do? Use the code on page 73 to check your answer.

⑦⑨❻⑤ ⑥⊃⊃④ ❹⊃
❹⑧⑤ ▼⑤⑤④❾

____

____

Double underline the words from the Bible that describe Stephen.

Prayer:
Dear God, please help me to discover the job you have for me in your big plan.

47 God's power

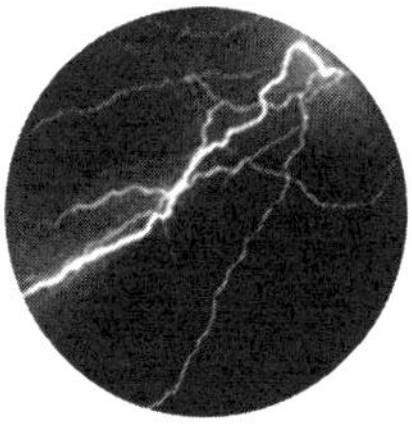

God is powerful.

But God doesn't always show his power in spectacular ways.

Do you remember the first man the church chose to organise the meals for the needy? Use the code wheel below to check your answer.

❸❹⑤➔⑧⑤▼

____

In the Bible bit look for a spectacular way and a more ordinary way the Holy Spirit showed his power in Stephen.

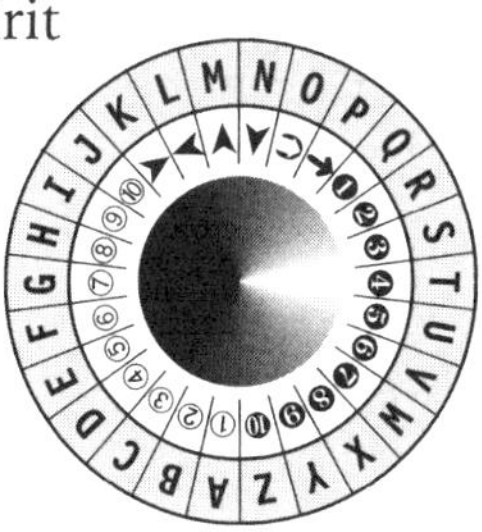

Acts 6:8-10

8 God gave Stephen the
power to work great miracles
and wonders among the
people. 9 But some men from
Cyrene and Alexandria were
members of a group who
called themselves "Free
Men." They started arguing
with Stephen. Some others
from Cilicia and Asia also
argued with him. 10 But they
were no match for Stephen,
who spoke with the great
wisdom that the Spirit gave
him.

It's the Holy Spirit's job to change us to be loving and fair always, like Jesus. What did people notice about the way Stephen spoke?

____

____

Prayer:
Dear God, please make me wise in what I say. Help me to know when to speak and when to be quiet. Give me courage when I feel afraid to speak. I want you to be pleased with everything I say.

48 Shining for God

Alana, Mei, Reuben, Suzy and Kate were playing around outside the garage waiting for Sean. They knew he would be late because he was running in the Little Athletics Carnival.

Soon Sean arrived. Before he said anything Kate congratulated him.

'How did you know I ran a personal best?' he asked.

'I can tell by your face!' Kate replied.

Acts 6:12-15

12 They all grabbed Stephen and dragged him in front of the council.

13 Some men agreed to tell lies about Stephen, and they said, "This man keeps on saying terrible things about this holy temple and the Law of Moses. 14 We have heard him claim that Jesus from Nazareth will destroy this place and change the customs that Moses gave us." 15 Then all the council members stared at Stephen. They saw that his face looked like the face of an angel.

Can you find out?

The leader's all time hero was Moses. After Moses had been with God something happened to his face. Find Exodus 34:29-30 in a Bible. What happened?

In the Bible bit today, Stephen's face had something to tell. *Circle the words that tell what it was like.*

What do you think the face of an angel looks like?

- loving
- angry
- disinterested
- strong
- shining

What would the leaders think of Stephen after that?

Prayer:
Lord God, please let my face and everything about me let others know how important you are to me.

49

Don't be stubborn

The Hotshots opened their Bibles to read the next bit about Stephen. They wanted to know if the leaders would listen to Stephen after his face shone.

Acts 7:51-53

51 (Stephen said) 'You stubborn
and hardheaded people! You
are always fighting against the
Holy Spirit, just as your
ancestors did. 52 Is there one
prophet that your ancestors
didn't mistreat? They killed
the prophets who told about
the coming of the One Who
Obeys God. And now you have
turned against him and killed
him. 53 Angels gave you God's
Law, but you still don't obey it.'

God was giving the leaders another opportunity to turn to him. They could be forgiven if they accepted Jesus.

Underline the words that describe the leaders.

Kate suggested everyone be still for a moment and ask themselves if they were being stubborn and refusing to listen to God. Then she prayed:

Prayer Idea:
You might like to pray the prayer Kate prayed with the Hotshots.

Jesus is still doing things in the world

A true story from Ethiopia

Ethiopia is a country in Africa. In the late 1900's the government told Christians they had to stop living for Jesus or go to prison. Over 20,000 were arrested. One of them was Tadesse Ayissa. He was put in prison and tortured for his faith.

'Stop believing and you will go free. If not, you will die,' the soldiers told him.

Tadesse would not give up his faith. He had to stand on his own and six or seven soldiers lined up to shoot him. The officer gave the order and the soldiers fired. Every bullet missed.

The officer was so shocked he didn't tell his soldiers to fire again. In fact he started thinking that Jesus must be alive and powerful to protect Tadesse like that.

The officer later became a Christian and so did many others.

From that time the church in Ethiopia grew stronger than ever.

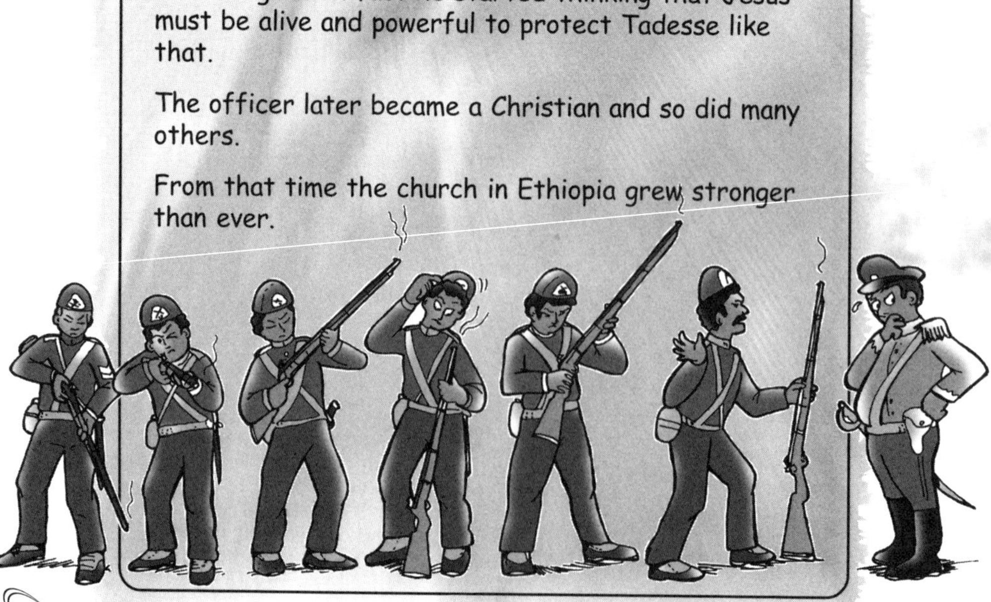

(Based on the video 'Window on Ethiopia' The Bible Society 1996)

50

Safe with God

Do you think the leaders will change their mind after Stephen's speech?

Acts 7:54-60

54 When the council members
heard Stephen's speech, they
were angry and furious. 55 But
Stephen was filled with the
Holy Spirit. He looked toward
heaven, where he saw our
glorious God and Jesus
standing at his right side.
56 Then Stephen said, "I see
heaven open and the Son of
Man standing at the right
side of God!"

57 The council members
shouted and covered their
ears. At once they all
attacked Stephen 58 and
dragged him out of the city.
Then they started throwing
stones at him. The men who
had brought charges against
him put their coats at the
feet of a young man named
Saul.

59 As Stephen was being
stoned to death, he called
out, "Lord Jesus, please
welcome me!" 60 He knelt down
and shouted, "Lord, don't
blame them for what they
have done." Then he died.

'That's not fair! Why didn't God save Stephen?' asked Alana. 'I thought if you believe, God looks after you.'

'What happened to Stephen?' asked Kate.

'They killed him and God didn't stop them!'

'And then what ?'

Alana stopped a moment. 'I guess he was safe with God in heaven,' she said quietly.

> God's plan is bigger than what happens on earth. He's working towards a new world where things will be perfect forever. Bad things happen now, even for those who love God very much, but nothing can keep us from God and God can turn the bad things into good.

Prayer idea:
Has something happened to you or someone you know that isn't fair? Talk to God about it. Ask him to turn it into something that will help his new world come. Ask him to help you trust him.

51 From bad to worse

Alana nodded and told Kate about how everyone at home was fighting.

'Sometimes it seems like God doesn't know or care,' Kate told her. 'When things like that happen I try to think bigger.'

'Bigger?'

'I think that God is taking care of me as well as working things out. I try not to get stuck in just what's happening now. One day those who love God will never be unhappy again.'

Life in the early church was dangerous. Read what was happening.

Acts 8:1-3

1-2 Saul approved the stoning of Stephen. Some faithful followers of the Lord buried Stephen and mourned very much for him.

At that time the church in Jerusalem suffered terribly. All of the Lord's followers, except the apostles, were scattered everywhere in Judea and Samaria. 3 Saul started making a lot of trouble for the church. He went from house to house, arresting men and women and putting them in jail.

Colour the shapes with a cross to see who was making trouble.

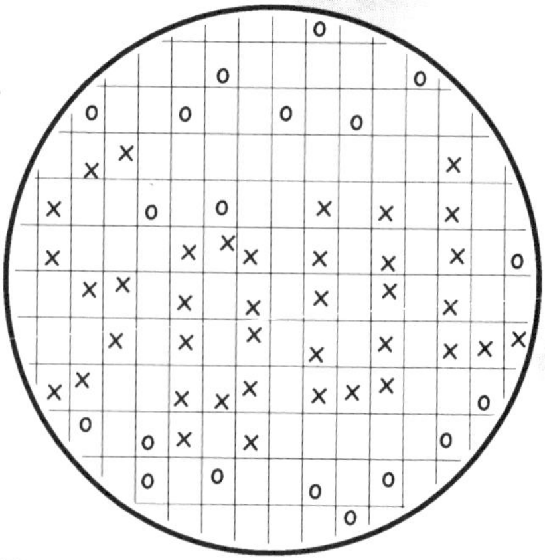

Prayer:
Please God, help me to trust you when things are awful. Help me to believe that you still love me when things are painful and sad as well as when things are great.

52 Spreading the message

Mei was bored.
'Nothing good ever happens around here,' she moaned.

Do you have days like that?

In the city of Samaria in Bible times there were people who thought nothing good ever happened to them. They weren't just bored. They were sick or troubled and they didn't know any way out.

When Saul started making trouble it was BAD NEWS for the Christians in Jerusalem. They ran away to other cities. Philip went to Samaria.

In Jerusalem there were lots of Christians who knew Jesus and the hope he gives.

That was GOOD NEWS for those who lived in Samaria. Philip brought the message about Jesus to them.

Acts 8:4-8

4 The Lord's followers who had been scattered went from place to place, telling the good news. 5 Philip went to the city of Samaria and told the people about Christ. 6 They crowded around Philip because they were eager to hear what he was saying and to see him work miracles. 7 Many people with evil spirits were healed, and the spirits went out of them with a shout. A lot of crippled and lame people were also healed. 8 Everyone in that city was very glad because of what was happening.

Underline the good things that happened in Samaria after Jesus' followers went there.

Time for another time-ship trip. Let's check out Samaria at the time of Philip!

Prayer:
Thank you God, that even when some things are bad you are working out your plans for good. Please help me to trust you and live for you.

King Omri, ruler of the Northern Kingdom of Israel built a new city on a hill and called it **Samaria**. He built walls all around to protect the city. But the walls weren't strong enough to keep out invading armies. In years to come, Samaria was wrecked many times.

King Herod cleaned up the mess from the destroyed city and built a palace for himself and beautiful new buildings in honour of false gods. He built a wall around the city more than four kilometres long. **Samaria** was an important and impressive city with towers, stadium and a huge theatre but people didn't know the truth about Jesus.

53 Other gods

Acts 8:9-13

[9] For some time a man named Simon had lived in the city of Samaria and had amazed the people. He practiced witchcraft and claimed to be somebody great.
[10] Everyone, rich and poor, crowded around him. They said, "This man is the power of God called 'The Great Power.' "

[11] For a long time, Simon had used witchcraft to amaze the people, and they kept crowding around him.
[12] But when they believed what Philip was saying about God's kingdom and about the name of Jesus Christ, they were all baptized.
[13] Even Simon believed and was baptized. He stayed close to Philip, because he marvelled at all the miracles and wonders.

People thought Simon was great and powerful, – a kind of god. They loved to watch him. He had power over them by the tricks he did. When they compared Simon with the truth about Jesus who did they decide to follow?

There are lots of 'gods' people follow. Some people spend all their time at sport. They hardly care about anything else. Sport is their 'god'.

Can you think of any other 'gods'?'

What's most important to you?

Is something taking the place of God? Think about it carefully.

Prayer:
Dear God. You are the greatest! Please help me never to think that anything matters more than you.

54 No short cuts

Acts 8:18-24

[18] Simon noticed that the Spirit was given only when the apostles placed their hands on the people. So he brought money [19] and said to Peter and John, "Let me have this power too! Then anyone I place my hands on will also be given the Holy Spirit."

[20] Peter said to him, "You and your money will both end up in hell if you think you can buy God's gift! [21] You don't have any part in this, and God sees that your heart isn't right. [22] Get rid of these evil thoughts and ask God to forgive you. [23] I can see that you are jealous and bound by your evil ways."

[24] Simon said, "Please pray to the Lord, so that what you said won't happen to me."

Sean used to read Hotshots before he went to bed but often he was too tired to think about God or pray. One day when he woke up early, he decided to change his Hotshots time to before school.

He remembered what Kate said, 'It's not just about reading and saying a quick prayer. It's about getting to know God and that takes time. There's no short cut.'

Sean wants to really know God well and be the sort of Christian who makes a difference in the world.

Simon in Samaria wanted to see God's power in his life like it was in the apostles. He thought there might be an easy way of getting it.

No short cuts continued ...

What did Simon offer the apostles? _ _ _ _ _

What did the apostles tell him?

❾➲❺❷ ⑧⑤①❷❹ ⑨❸▼❹ ❷⑨⑦⑧❹

_ _ _ _ _ _ _ _ _ _ _ _ _ _ _, _ _ _ _ _ _

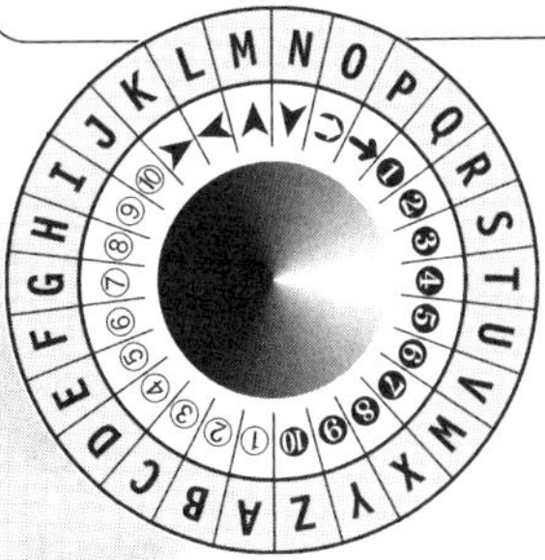

Simon said he believed, but he was thinking the wrong way. He wasn't trying to please God at all. He was after more power for himself.

The Hotshots and Kate decided to make a chart of ways of telling if they were thinking right.

Prayer idea:
There's something we can do when we know our heart isn't right. God is ready to forgive us when we turn to him in prayer. Now is a good time to do it.

55 Spreading the message

If you had a message for the whole world, how would you tell it?

- TV?
- Internet?
- Laser lights in the sky?

The first Christians had the good news about Jesus to tell the whole world. How could they do it? Horses and camels were about the fastest way of spreading news.

Read about God's brilliant way of getting the message to Africa. By chariot!

Acts 8:26-31

26 The Lord's angel said to Philip, "Go south
along the desert road that leads from
Jerusalem to Gaza." 27 So Philip left.
An important Ethiopian official happened
to be going along that road in his chariot.
He was the chief treasurer for Candace,
the Queen of Ethiopia. The official had
gone to Jerusalem to worship 28 and was
now on his way home. He was sitting in his
chariot, reading the book of the prophet
Isaiah.

29 The Spirit told Philip to catch up with
the chariot. 30 Philip ran up close and heard
the man reading aloud from the book of
Isaiah. Philip asked him, "Do you
understand what you are reading?"

31 The official answered, "How can I
understand unless someone helps me?"
He then invited Philip to come up and sit
beside him.

Who do you know who could answer your questions about God?

- grandparent
- mum or dad
- someone at church
- Sunday school teacher

Don't be shy! They'll probably be very glad you asked.

Something to do

Ask someone to help you find Ethiopia on a map.

How long do you think it would take to get there from Jerusalem if you had a chariot?

Prayer:

Dear God, thank you for giving us people who can help us understand about you. Help me to share what I know about you too.

56 Philip explains

The Ethiopian in the chariot could read his Bible but he didn't know what it meant. The words were about someone Philip knew well, in fact someone who was living in him by his Spirit! See if you know when you read it.

Acts 8:32-35

32 The man was reading the passage that said,
"He was led like a sheep
on its way to be killed.
He was silent as a lamb
whose wool
is being cut off,
and he did not say
a word.
33 He was treated like a nobody
and did not receive
a fair trial.
How can he have children,
if his life
is snatched away?"

34 The official said to Philip, "Tell me,
was the prophet talking about himself or
about someone else?" 35 So Philip began
at this place in the Scriptures and
explained the good news about Jesus.

Underline the words about Jesus.

Suzy was very quiet. She was thinking about Jesus when he was arrested and killed. It was hard to think of the powerful Son of God being as helpless as a lamb. She was very glad he died for her.

Prayer:
Think about Jesus and all he did for you. Tell him how you feel about what he did.

57 Do something about it!

Suzy went home after Hotshots and thought some more about Jesus. She felt she'd never really understood about Jesus dying for her before. She felt sad. 'I'm really sorry, Jesus,' she whispered. She felt she loved him so much she would do anything for him. She wrote a prayer in her special notebook.

She wanted to make sure she didn't forget, so she decided to take her notebook to show Kate.

Kate read the notebook and told Suzy,

'That's great! I'm glad you wrote that prayer. As soon as the others get here we'll read about someone else who did something as soon as he understood about Jesus.'

Acts 8:36-40

36-37 As they were going along
the road, they came to a place
where there was some water.
The official said, "Look! Here
is some water. Why can't I be
baptized?" 38 He ordered the
chariot to stop. Then they both
went down into the water, and
Philip baptized him.

39 After they had come out of
the water, the Lord's Spirit
took Philip away. The official
never saw him again, but he was
very happy as he went on his
way.

40 Philip later appeared in
Azotus. He went from town to
town, all the way to Caesarea,
telling people about Jesus.

Prayer idea:
Do you always pray the same way? Some children like to *say* their prayers aloud. Others *think* their prayers inside their head.

Suzy *wrote* her special prayer. Sometimes it's good to *sing* prayers.

What do you want to say to God today? You might like to write it on a piece of paper, like Suzy.

Pray it differently to the way you usually do.

The Holy Spirit

The Hotshots remembered some things they read in the Bible. Look back through this book and think about what you know. Write your own list in the box.

Here's some verses to help you remember what they Holy Spirit did.

Genesis 1:1-2

Acts 1:8

Acts 2:4

Acts 2:38

Acts 4:31

Acts 6:5

Use the code for a message about the Holy Spirit.

❹⑧⑤ ⑧⊃◀❾ ❸→⑨❷⑨❹ ⑨❸ ⑨▼❻⑨❸⑨②◀⑤

___ ____ _____ __ __________

❹⑧⑤ ⑧⊃◀❾ ❸→⑨❷⑨❹ ⑨❸ ⑦⊃④

___ ____ _____ __ ___

❹⑧⑤ ⑧⊃◀❾ ❸→⑨❷⑨❹ ◀⑨❻⑤❸
⑨▼ ⑩⑤❸❺❸' ⑥⊃◀◀⊃❼⑤❷❸

___ ____ _____ _____ __ _____' _________

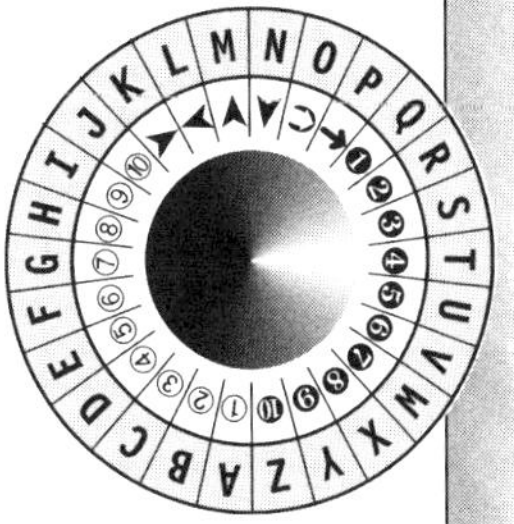

58 The Holy Spirit and us

After the Hotshots talked about the Holy Spirit, Suzy said...

Underline the parts in the Bible bit that are like Suzy's note.

John 14:15-17

15 Jesus said to his disciples:

If you love me, you will do as I command. 16 Then I will ask the Father to send you the Holy Spirit who will help you and always be with you. 17 The Spirit will show you what is true. The people of this world cannot accept the Spirit, because they don't see or know him. But you know the Spirit, who is with you and will keep on living in you.

Suzy pulled out her special notebook. Here's what she wrote

Prayer:
Dear God, thank you for your Holy Spirit.
I specially want to thank you that the Holy Spirit

____

____

(Make up your own ending).

59 When others don't believe

Reuben was late but when he arrived he had plenty to tell the others.

Reuben continued, 'They stood all around me. When they laughed I told them, "You don't know anything. I know God's real!" Then they just looked while I walked away. I couldn't believe it.'

From the very beginning of the church, believers have been hassled. Jesus warned his followers it would happen. He said they might even be killed.

John 16:1-4

I am telling you this to keep you from being afraid. 2 You will be chased out of the Jewish meeting places. And the time will come when people will kill you and think they are doing God a favour. 3 They will do these things because they don't know either the Father or me. 4 I am saying this to you now, so that when the time comes, you will remember what I have said.

Who lives in us to help us when things like that happen?

_ _ _   _ _ _ _   _ _ _ _ _ _

Prayer:
Please God, help everyone who is in trouble just because they believe in you. Make them brave to say and do what you want, even when it's dangerous.

60 For the whole world

'Wouldn't it be good if those bullies came to Hotshots?' said Kate.

'Maybe not now,' Kate told him, 'but the Holy Spirit can change all that. Let's read what Jesus said about it.'

John 16:8-11

8 The Spirit will come and show the people of this world the truth about sin and God's justice and the judgment. 9 The Spirit will show them that they are wrong about sin, because they didn't have faith in me. 10 They are wrong about God's justice, because I am going to the Father, and you won't see me again. 11 And they are wrong about the judgment, because God has already judged the ruler of this world.

What will the Spirit do for those who don't believe in Jesus (the people of this world)?

❸⑧➲❼ ❹⑧⑤▲ ❹⑧⑤❾ ①❷⑤
❼❷➲▼⑦ ①▼④ ⑩⑤❸❺❸ ⑨❸
❹❷❺⑤

____ ____ ____ ___

_____ ___ _____ __ ____

Prayer:
Lord God, I pray for people who don't know the truth about Jesus. I pray that when the Holy Spirit shows them the truth, they will believe and follow Jesus.

God is doing

What have you seen God doing in the world lately?
Are yo
him c
throug

chings in the rld

tting
nings
ou?

How to ask Jesus

We all need a Saviour.

We've all done bad things and gone against God. (Even if we don't mean to.)

Jesus is the only one who can save us from the wrong that we do.

to be your Saviour

If you have never asked Jesus to be your Saviour, you can ask him now.

The first steps

1 Thank you

Say thank you to God for loving you and promising to forgive you. Thank Jesus for coming to save you.

2 Sorry

Tell God you are sorry for the sin and wrong in your life. Ask God to save you from it.

3 Please

Ask God to give you a new start. Ask for the Holy Spirit's help you live a new life, doing what Jesus wants you to do.

e loved
s so much
that he
died on
the cross
to save
us.

Make up your own prayer using **THANK YOU**, **SORRY**, **PLEASE**. You might like to write it on a piece of paper before you pray it.

Write the date you prayed this prayer:

CERTIFICATE

Scripture Union and The hotshots

This is to certify that

. . . .

. . . .

(write your name neatly)

has completed the stories and projects from...

The time everything EXPLODED with ENERGY

Signed: kate ....

Kate (Hotshots Leader)

Countersigned: ....

(Parent or other adult)

Date: ....